Pope Francis

Portrait of Holiness

a tribute by *Judie Brown*

Pope Francis

Copyright © 2013 by Judie Brown
Published by: American Life League

All rights reserved, including the right to reproduce this book or portions thereof in any form whatsoever. For information or to obtain permission contact:

American Life League
P.O. Box 1350, Stafford, VA 22555
www.all.org

miserando atque eligendo

Manufactured in the United States of America
Cover design and book layout by: Carlos J. Carbo

ISBN 978-0-9896075-0-6

Portrait of Holiness: Pope Francis

Approaching the preparation of a manuscript on the subject of our new Holy Father, Pope Francis, is like putting a toe in the water of the ocean and hesitating to go into the deep. His reputation and his repeated calls over the years for justice for all human beings—born and preborn—are legendary in Argentina and at the Vatican. So much has already been reported about him that one might think there is nothing left to say.

So what can I write about him that will be refreshing and new? This booklet is my attempt to share insight into how his statements and writings fit like a glove with those of his predecessors. Such teachings are constant and true. Their messages call each of us to strive to inspire a new beginning, a renewed respect for life, and a message of hope to our brothers and sisters—both born and preborn.

Defending innocent human beings should be the mission of each and every Catholic. Hopefully this small volume will help those who doubt the need for their witness to the dignity of the human being see that every one of us has a contribution to make.

For American Life League, the road to defending Catholic teaching with greater clarity had a definitive beginning. I recall vividly that wonderful day in March of 1995 when Pope John Paul II issued his historic encyclical letter, *Evangelium Vitae (The Gospel of Life)*. We were excited, to put it mildly, and could not wait to read it cover to cover, and then read it again and again.

As we pondered the bounty of teaching contained in that encyclical, the staff of American Life League agreed that we must prepare, and then deliver to the Holy Father, a set of study guides on this magnificent message that would make *The Gospel of Life* come alive for anyone interested in studying it, whether he be a commuter, a Bible scholar, or a student. We prepared four small books dealing with this encyclical and, in addition, added a small one on the 1993 encyclical *Veritatis Splendor (The Splendor of Truth)*. The reason for this addition was quite simple, actually, because once we understood Pope John Paul II's message we knew that only with a foundation in "the splendor of truth" would anyone properly appreciate *The Gospel of Life*.

We travelled to Rome that October and, in a few moments so memorable they are vividly etched in my memory, we presented those study guides to the Holy Father. When we got home, we published and marketed all five. It was a glorious year indeed.

And just a few short months later, with the Holy Father's blessing, I was selected to serve on the Pontifical Academy for Life. It was an honor and a blessing to be part of that august body for three consecutive five-year terms. Over those 15 years, I grew in understanding and appreciation of Catholic teaching on matters relating to the human person. That experience, among others, prepared me for the preparation of this volume.

The pro-life apostolate worldwide has been inspired so often by Church documents, in particular Pope John Paul II's *Letter to Families (Familiaris Consortio), The Splendor of Truth, The Gospel of Life,* and the beautiful encyclical on the Eucharist. We have also been blessed to share several of the writings of Pope Benedict XVI, including his paper on the formation of conscience and his renowned memorandum entitled *Worthiness to Receive Holy Communion,* among others.[1]

While there have been many more, these are the documents that set the stage for Pope Francis and his own writings and speeches. Everything that he accomplished prior to his election to the Chair of Peter and, we pray, onward suggests to us that his pontificate will be glorious.

Our goal is to help others capture the vision that will drive us forward in our quest to restore moral sanity to our nation and to the world.

Dedication

With humble gratitude for his teaching and inspiration, I dedicate this work to the memory of Blessed John Paul II.

Pope Francis

Holiness: What does it mean?

The Catechism of the Catholic Church defines holiness in these words: "Charity is the soul of the holiness to which all are called: It 'governs, shapes, and perfects all the means of sanctification.'" [2]

The *Catechism* gives this simple explanation of how we pursue sanctity in our daily lives and suggests we reflect on this writing from the pen of St. Therese of Lisieux, the Little Flower: [3]

> Charity gave me the key to my vocation. I understood that if the Church had a body composed of different members, the most necessary and most noble of all could not be lacking to it, and so I understood that the Church had a heart and that this heart was burning with love. I understood that it was love alone that made the Church's members act, that if love were ever extinguished, apostles would not proclaim the gospel and martyrs would refuse to shed their blood. I understood that love includes all vocations. . . . Then in the excess of my delirious joy, I cried out: "O Jesus, my Love . . . at last I have found my vocation; my vocation is Love!"

Pope Francis reflects this same type of holiness in his manner and through his words. When he addressed the media for the first time on Saturday, March 16, 2013, he reminded Catholics that it is Jesus, not the pope, who is at the center of the Church—a Church he said should be "poor, and for the poor."[4]

The pope further explained his choice of the name Francis, saying, "He [St. Francis of Assisi] was a man of poverty, peace, and [he] safeguarded creation . . . He is the man who gives us this spirit of peace, the poor man."[5] He reminded the journalists that the Catholic Church is a spiritual body, not a political body—a "holy people of God who walk toward the encounter with Jesus Christ." Further, he stated that, the only way to "fully explain how the Catholic Church works" is by putting yourself in this perspective. Pope Francis emphasized that "Christ is the center . . . the heart of the Church! Without Him, neither Peter nor the Church would exist or have a reason for being."

The Holy Father's emphasis on being always aware that it is Christ, not you or me or the pope, who is the central focus of our faith, reminds us of the prophetic words of the St. John the Apostle who said, "He must increase, I must decrease."

On Sunday, March 17, during his homily which focused on the gospel story (John 8: 2-10) of the adulterous woman the Pharisees wanted to stone, Pope Francis explained the stark differences among those who came to hear and to see Jesus in those days,[6]

> There is also a difference among the people: There are the people who went with him; he sat down and began to teach them: The people who wanted to hear Jesus' words, the people with open hearts, in need of the Word of God. There were others, who heard nothing, they could not hear; and they are those who brought the woman: Listen, Master, here is one, and one that . . . We must do to her what Moses commanded us to do to these women (cf. 8:4-5).

> We too believe that we are these people, who, on the one hand want to listen to Jesus, but, on the

other hand, we like to cudgel others, to condemn others. And Jesus' message is mercy. For me, I say this humbly, it is the strongest message of the Lord—mercy. But he himself said it: I have not come for the just; the just justify themselves. Go ahead, blessed Lord, if you can do it, I cannot! But they think that they can do it. I have come for sinners (cf. Mark 2:17).

These are the words of a man whose humility and holiness are not readily apparent because he does not call attention to them. Rather, he reflects—or might I say radiates—those gifts that make him a portrait of holiness. The Catholic Church is blessed.

How it all began: Argentina's spiritual leader elected to the Chair of Peter

A new era in the papacy began on March 13, 2013, with the election of Argentina's cardinal, Jorge Bergoglio. He is the 266th pope of the Roman Catholic Church. He is the first pope of the Americas, the first Jesuit to be elected pope, and the first pope to choose the name Francis.[7]

Pope Francis was born on December 17, 1936, in Argentina to Italian immigrants.[8] He grew up among five siblings and learned the values instilled in him by his parents, which today define him as a simple man of God.

He earned a chemical technician's diploma in secondary school before discerning that he had a vocation to the priesthood. He entered the Society of Jesus in 1958 and was ordained into the Catholic priesthood in 1969. He was elevated to cardinal in 2001 by Pope John Paul II, and has had a laudable career as leader of Argentina's more than 30 million Catholics (92 percent of Argentina's population).⁹ While this sounds amazing, the truth is that only 20 percent of them are active in the Church.

Though that statistic is a sad commentary on our day, Pope Francis is surely a witness to the fact that these are the times for a vicar of Christ on earth who loves all people, including the poorest of the poor. If it is true that hardened hearts are touched by the reflections of Christ's love seen in man's public witness, then surely Pope Francis will provide leadership for one and all.

The Holy Father's humility is apparent in the words he spoke to his fellow cardinals immediately after his election to the papacy: "I am a great sinner confident in the patience and mercy of God. In suffering, I accept."[10]

You and I find such words amazing. But for those who used to attend the Masses then-Cardinal Bergoglio celebrated in a local Buenos Aires neighborhood near the 126 bus stop, his loving, humble manner was always apparent.[11] One writer called Pope Francis "a father for everyone." Julio, a security guard at the Vatican, added, "I believe . . . that he is the right man to . . . build a foundation for a merciful community that understands how to forgive and to fight for equality for all."

Deacon Keith Fournier wrote about the first appearance of the Holy Father before those gathered in St. Peter's Square:[12]

> Pope Francis did something which astounded me. He asked the faithful—before he gave them the *Urbi et Orbi* [to the city and to the world] Apostolic blessing—to pray for him. He bowed before those assembled in the square during a

moment of silence. That was profoundly moving and, I suggest, telling. . . .

The Lord uses holy and humble men at critical times in Church history to bring authentic renewal. May the pope who bears the name of Francis exhibit the humility, deep prayer, and level of spiritual gifts which his namesake offered at another critical time in the history of the Church and the world.

The Holy Father's manner has been recognized the world over by prominent leaders such as Israeli president Shimon Peres who "said that Pope Francis 'represents the devotion, the love of God, the love of peace, the holy modesty, and he represents a new continent which is now awakening.'"[13]

Pope Francis: Apostle of truth

Prior to his election, then-Cardinal Jorge Bergoglio had a clear understanding of what was needed within the Church herself for the healing that must precede evangelization in the world.

In 2005, Bergoglio delivered an address to religious in which he talked frankly about the need to deal honestly with one's own sins prior to setting out to "correct" those in others. He exposed the problematic nature of arrogance and haughty disregard for brotherly love and how such defective behavior displaces humility and self-awareness of imperfections with pain and sorrow.

Though he was addressing the proper formation of individuals preparing for the religious life and the priesthood, his words apply to everyone who wishes to imitate Christ in daily life.

He said:[14]

> Factions fighting to impose . . . their own viewpoint and preferences are fairly common in religious communities, both local and provincial. This occurs when charitable openness to neighbor is replaced by each individual's own ideas. It is no longer the religious family as a whole, which the religious defends, but only the part of it that concerns him. People no longer adhere to the unity that contributes to configuring the Body of Christ, but rather to the divisive, distorting, and debilitating conflict. . . . One of the effective attitudes that must acquire substance in the hearts of young religious is that of "self-accusation."

The Holy Father was encouraging among those to whom he was speaking a humble awareness that each human being has flaws. In the context of the human family or any relationship that we might have with others, "self-accusation" represents our ability to admit when we are wrong, to embrace with love and charity those who offend us, and to live our lives as a reflection of Christ's life. This takes a special kind of courage that enables us to let our true selves shine through, even when it is uncomfortable for us to do so.

Bergoglio's wisdom carried forward from Argentina to the Vatican and, in fact, to the meetings the cardinals from around the world had prior to electing the next pope. In preparation for a talk then-Cardinal Bergoglio was scheduled to give the cardinals, he wrote an outline in which he addressed the apostolic zeal required of those who are called to evangelize on behalf of Christ and His Church.

Once he was elected, he agreed to have those notes made public. In them he noted that, in order for evangelization to be effective, "the Church is called to come out of herself and to go to the peripheries" whether doing so around the world or in the spiritual realm including "the mystery of sin, of pain, of injustice, of ignorance and indifference to religion, of intellectual currents, and of all misery."[15]

Using the example of the crippled woman in Luke 13:11, Bergoglio noted that, when the Church does not come out of herself in the act of evangelization, she is like the woman in the gospel. He called this ailment a type of "theological narcissism," meaning a certain attitude among some of the Church's members and leaders that exhibits itself as a worldly kind of spirituality. In essence, this means that where such a condition exists, the Church becomes ill and unable to go out into the world, teaching and preaching Christ as she should. In Bergoglio's words: "In Revelation, Jesus says that He is at the door and knocks. Obviously, the text refers to His knocking from the outside in order to enter but I think about the times in which Jesus knocks from within so that we will let Him come out. The self-referential Church keeps Jesus Christ within herself and does not let Him out."

The stark contrast between the Church evangelizing IN the world and the Church that is self-absorbed amazes those who can see the challenges confronting the Church today. In order for souls to be won to Christ, the Church must first examine her own failures and reform in those areas where problems have arisen due to lack of humility and internal examination.

Bergoglio was speaking at that time about the type of man he believed should be elected pope, and it is interesting that he wrote this in his outline: "He must be a man who, from the contemplation and adoration of Jesus Christ, helps the Church to go out to the existential peripheries, that helps her to be the fruitful mother, who gains life from 'the sweet and comforting joy of evangelizing.'" These words call to mind the profound words of Pope John Paul II in his letter on the family: "The whole Church is obliged to a deep reflection and commitment, so that the new culture now emerging may be evangelized in depth, true values acknowledged, the rights of men and women defended, and justice promoted in the very structures of society. In this way the 'new humanism' will not distract people from their relationship with God, but will lead them to it more fully."[16]

Pope John Paul II watched the culture of death beginning to swallow families as it attempted to tempt children with all manner of bad behavior and, sadly, their parents as well. He knew then what Pope Francis is saying now. A healthy, robust, holy Church can solve these problems; a sick Church cannot.

Then-Cardinal Bergoglio's special perspective on the Church and her needs today were fulfilled by his own election to the pontificate—a need he is more than well-suited to fill.

Pope Francis: Jesuit

Pope Francis is the first Jesuit ever to be elected to the Chair of Peter. When the superior general of the Jesuits, Father Adolfo Nicolás, sent a letter of congratulations to the pope, the Holy Father reciprocated with his own letter. In that letter he breathed a bit of fresh air into our impression of Jesuits these days, calling on them to be "evangelical leaven" to the Church.

He wrote:[17]

Dear Father Nicolás,

I received with great joy the kind letter you sent me, in your name and that of the Society of Jesus, on the occasion of my election to the See of Peter, in which you assure me of your prayers for me and my apostolic ministry as well as your full disposition to continue serving—unconditionally—the Church and the vicar of Christ according to the teachings of St. Ignatius Loyola. My heartfelt thanks for this sign of affection and closeness, which I am happy to reciprocate, asking the Lord to illuminate and accompany all Jesuits, so that faithful to the charism received and following in the footsteps of the saints of our beloved Order, they may be evangelical leaven in the world in their pastoral action, but above all in the witness of a life totally dedicated to the service of the Church, the spouse of Christ, seeking unceasingly the glory of God and the good of souls.

With these sentiments, I ask all Jesuits to pray for me and to entrust me to the loving protection of the Virgin Mary, our Mother in heaven, while as a sign of God's abundant graces, I give you the Apostolic Blessing with special affection, which I also extend to all those who cooperate with the Society of Jesus in her activities, those who benefit from her good deeds and participate in her spirituality.

This is a great blessing for all of us. The elite centers of Catholic higher education that are identified with the Jesuit order are badly in need of a return to fidelity to the

Church and her teaching so that the "leaven" to which the pope refers may rise and spread.

Patrick Reilly, the leader of the renowned Cardinal Newman Society—the go-to source on learning where the good Catholic colleges are and where the problems exist—wrote shortly after Pope Francis' election,[18]

> Too often, today's graduates from Jesuit universities identify as "Catholic" but have little regard for the pope, the bishops, the sacraments, or Catholic moral teaching—outside of social justice concerns.
>
> So is it folly to hope for the renewal of Jesuit education?
>
> We don't think so, and many Jesuits would strongly agree. Now, with a Jesuit at the Vatican, Pope Francis could have an important influence.

Pope Francis and the saint from Assisi

Everything we have seen so far leads us to believe that Pope Francis chose his name because of an inspiration from the Holy Spirit. Lest we forget, St. Francis of Assisi was also confronted with problems in the Church during his time. The saint heard the voice of Christ saying: "Francis, repair my Church, which has fallen into disrepair!"[19]

Johann Christoph Arnold explains, "At first he took this commandment literally, thinking he was to rebuild broken walls and stonework. But he soon came to understand that God was calling him to something much more—to call his fellow believers back to the radical simplicity of the gospel."

Portrait of Holiness

Like St. Francis of Assisi, Pope Francis is in love with the Church and with the truths contained in her magisterium. He wants to lead the Church to be poor in spirit, to embrace the marginalized, and to spread the good news. In his inaugural Mass homily he made this very plain when he said:[20]

> Jesus Christ conferred power upon Peter, but what sort of power was it? Jesus' three questions to Peter about love are followed by three commands: Feed my lambs, feed my sheep. Let us never forget that authentic power is service, and that the pope too, when exercising power, must enter ever more fully into that service which has its radiant culmination on the Cross. He must be inspired by the lowly, concrete, and faithful service which marked Saint Joseph and, like him, he must open his arms to protect all of God's people and embrace with tender affection the whole of humanity, especially the poorest, the weakest, the least important, those whom Matthew lists in the final judgment on love—the hungry, the thirsty, the stranger, the naked, the sick and those in prison (cf. Mt 25:31-46). Only those who serve with love are able to protect!

What else can we say about the man who chose the name Francis?

Pope Francis: Apostle of love
A Jesuit journey toward sharing Christ's love in truth

In his very first words, Pope Francis set a tone: "And now let us begin this journey, the bishop and the people, this journey of the Church of Rome which presides in charity over all the Churches, a journey of brotherhood in love, of mutual trust. Let us always pray for one another."[21]

Catholic writer Helen Hull Hitchcock reflected on his use of the word "journey" and wrote that as Jesuit Saint Francis Xavier had done hundreds of years earlier, Pope Francis has embarked on a journey that will "consume his entire life." In this Year of Faith, his will be "a journey of obedience to a call to evangelize: To bring the message of love and truth of Jesus Christ to the far reaches of the world."

So true. The more one reads of his life as a Jesuit priest, the more one senses that our new pope was prepared by Christ for this historic event throughout his priesthood.

On Holy Thursday, Pope Francis joined a few priests for lunch after the Chrism Mass. Msgr. Enrico Feroci, the director of Caritas Rome, was present at the encounter and he spoke to Vatican radio.[22] Feroci explained that listening to the pope and being in his presence is "an extraordinary experience." Not only that, but he said the pope put everyone at ease.

During his conversation with these priests, Pope Francis said, "'Open the doors of the Church, and then the people will come in . . . if you keep the light on in the confessional and are available, then you will see what kind of line there is for confession.' . . . The pope said he was confident of the need of the people of God for priests to open the doors and allow the people to meet God."

Father Mario Pasquale, who had served as a worker-priest for 40 years, told Vatican Radio that he felt "heard" during the meal with the pope, and that he had the "feeling of being understood." Pasquale said Pope Francis told the priests that, as bishop of Rome, he wants to meet the people of the parishes. He continued, "You feel that the pope has a lot of hope in his heart. . . . I had this feeling that this is someone who loves the Church and invites you to love the Church, too, to the end—for life—and that it's worth it."

Pope Francis' love for the Church is legend in Argentina, as is his compassionate embrace of suffering persons including AIDS patients. We have read much about his dedication to the same principles that drove St. Francis of Assisi, most importantly reflecting Christ in charity. There is no doubt that this is a pope who will do much more than speak the teachings of the Church.

Pope Francis: Loving the dignity of the human person

Pope Francis' devotion to the sanctity of life and its defense cannot be overstated. His devotion to Church teaching is perhaps one of the many things that defines him as a true man of God—first and foremost a holy priest.

Here is one report that makes my point. In 2005, Catholic News Agency reported:[23]

> The archbishop of Buenos Aires, Cardinal Jorge Bergoglio, encouraged Catholics this week to untiringly defend the unborn against abortion even if "they persecute or kill you." Amidst a debate in the country over the legalization of abortion being sought by non-governmental organizations and by some members of the government, Cardinal Bergoglio recalled that the faithful have the duty to defend life "from the beginning until the end."

Catholics should persevere in this mission, he said, even if "they persecute you, calumniate you, set traps for you, take you to court, or kill you."

Such encouragement to heroically defend the intrinsic human right to life cannot go unnoticed, especially in our day of decriminalized abortion. Like his predecessors, Pope Francis calls us to love God and His children even more than we love our own lives. This is the height of selfless love, of imitating Christ.

The pope's sentiments and honesty about the zeal required of us as we strive to defend life echoes the beautiful words of Pope John Paul II who understood that being pro-life is the essence of living out our faith, no matter what the cost: "There are situations of acute poverty, anxiety, or frustration in which the struggle to make ends meet, the presence of unbearable pain, or instances of violence, especially against women, make the choice to defend and promote life so demanding as sometimes to reach the point of heroism."[24]

According to LifeSiteNews,[25]

At a Mass in Buenos Aires on Aug. 31, 2005, in honor of St. Raymond Nonnatus (Raymond "the unborn"), who is revered as the holy protector of pregnant women, the then-cardinal said that promoting life is "a road that is full of wolves."

"Perhaps for that reason they might bring us to the courts. Perhaps, for that reason, for caring for life, they might kill us," he said. "We should think about the Christian martyrs. They killed them for preaching this gospel of life, this gospel that Jesus brought. But Jesus gives us the strength."

The future pontiff also urged the faithful to "be astute" in promoting the gospel of life. "Go forth!

> Don't be fools," he said. "Remember, a Christian doesn't have the luxury of being foolish.
>
> . . . He can't give himself the luxury. He has to be clever, he has to be astute, to carry this out."

The fact that then-Cardinal Bergoglio chose the feast day of St. Raymond Nonnatus to give his people such inspirational words is no accident. St. Raymond was born in Portella, Catalonia, Spain in 1204.[26] His mother died in childbirth, and he was delivered via cesarean section (earning him the name non natus—meaning not born), yet he survived and went on to become, shortly before his death, a cardinal in the Church. He died in 1240 and, when he was canonized a saint, became the patron saint of expectant mothers and midwives. How appropriate it was that the Holy Father chose St. Raymond's feast day.

Pope Francis is an inspired writer and, in his 2011 book *Sobre el cielo y la tierra* (*On heaven and earth*), he wrote this about abortion:[27]

> The moral problem of abortion is of a pre-religious nature because the genetic code is written in a person at the moment of conception [i.e., creation]. A human being is there. I separate the topic of abortion from any specifically religious notions. It is a scientific problem. Not to allow the further development of a being which already has all the genetic code of a human being is not ethical. The right to life is the first among human rights. To abort a child is to kill someone who cannot defend himself.

As if his heart for the preborn child were not enough, then-Cardinal Bergoglio also had strong words for those priests who refuse to baptize the children of single mothers:[28]

> In our ecclesiastical region there are priests who don't baptize the children of single mothers because they weren't conceived in the sanctity of marriage. . . . These are today's hypocrites. Those who clericalize the Church. Those who separate the people of God from salvation. And this poor girl who, rather than returning the child to sender, had the courage to carry it into the world, must wander from parish to parish so that it's baptized!

For every single mother who has made the courageous choice to carry her pregnancy to term, these are words of love like no other. Such strong expressions of devotion to the gift of life and the heroism of expectant mothers who, against all odds, choose life for their babies endear the Holy Father to us. He is a beacon of hope in our troubled world.

Pope Francis has been very clear in his disdain and condemnation of the act of abortion, at one point calling it the "death penalty."[29]

We know that in our own country today his accurate definition of what the act of abortion actually is would earn derision; those who promote abortion would scoff, and yet it is this type of clear teaching that has already defined our beloved new pope.

I also have to say how much I loved reading that, after his election, the Holy Father used his second blessing for an expectant mother and her preborn child.[30] His action lit up the crowd! In doing that, the pope sent a clear message that he is united in solidarity with the child, the family, and the teachings of the Church on the question of respect for human dignity.

Having said all this, his most profound words came during his homily at the inaugural Mass:[31]

> The vocation of being a "protector," however, is not just something involving us Christians alone; it also has a prior dimension which is simply human, involving everyone. It means protecting all creation, the beauty of the created world, as the book of Genesis tells us and as Saint Francis of Assisi showed us. It means respecting each of God's creatures and respecting the environment in which we live. It means protecting people, showing loving concern for each and every person, especially children, the elderly, those in need, who are often the last we think about. It means caring for one another in our families: Husbands and wives first protect one another, and then, as parents, they care for their children, and children themselves, in time, protect their parents. It means building sincere friendships in which we protect one another in trust, respect, and goodness. In the end, everything has been entrusted to our protection, and all of us are responsible for it. Be protectors of God's gifts!

Be protectors! Music to our ears, isn't it?

His words and his acts of love toward mothers and their children echo so much of what Pope John Paul II conveyed to us during his 25 years as our spiritual leader. He wrote, "The deepest element of God's commandment to protect human life is the requirement to show reverence and love for every person and the life of every person."[32]

Remember Pope Benedict XVI's reminder to us: "Man is not a lost atom in a random universe: He is God's creature, whom God chose to endow with an immortal soul and whom he has always loved."[33]

St. Paul told the Romans this very same thing when he said: "Love is the one thing that cannot hurt your neighbor; that is why it is the answer to every one of the commandments."[34]

When we bask in such beautiful truths about the value of the human person and the unconditional love that is required of each of us as we work to defend life, we are blessed. Yet we also understand the challenge. Respect for the dignity of the human person has cried out for recognition and protection since the beginning of time. Yet in our age of sexual satisfaction and callous disregard for life and love, we are challenged as never before.

It is only in our walk with Christ that we find the courage to continue, and that is the message Pope Francis is sharing with us in word and deed.

Let us pray:

Lord, help us to remember that without You we can do nothing and with You all things are possible. May we, through Your grace and power and the intercession of St. Raymond Nonnatus, bring many souls to truth. We ask this in the powerful name of Jesus.

Amen.

Pope Francis loves the Eucharist

At the Last Supper, when Christ instituted the sacrament of the Eucharist, He gave a great gift to the Church and to each Catholic. This sacrament—the body, blood, soul, and divinity of Christ truly present—has been called the source and summit of our Catholic life.

Portrait of Holiness

The Holy Father has been teaching this very same message for many years. Then-Cardinal Bergoglio was speaking at a Eucharistic congress in 2012, when he said, "Mary's deep relationship with the Eucharist can guide the faithful and allow people to get closer to God. . . . She is the 'model of the bond between the Lord and his bride, the Church, between God and each man.'"[35]

The reporter who covered Cardinal Bergoglio's address concluded his report saying, "For Cardinal Bergoglio, the Eucharist must be at the center of the Church. Describing the Eucharist as the 'source and at the same time the summit of all evangelization' and a force that purifies and sanctifies the Church, the cardinal said that the bond between the Eucharist and the Church is one that cannot be broken."

Five years earlier, Cardinal Bergoglio, recognized as one of the chief leaders of the Catholic Church in Latin America, issued a joint statement on the Eucharist. In it we find these words:[36] "We should commit ourselves to 'Eucharistic coherence,' that is, we should be conscious that people cannot receive Holy Communion and at the same time act or speak against the commandments, in particular when abortions, euthanasia, and other serious crimes against life and family are facilitated. This responsibility applies particularly to legislators, governors, and health professionals."

In other words, if a Catholic is willfully breaking a commandment of God and committing a mortal sin, that Catholic should not receive the Eucharist until he has gone to confession. On the other hand, if that Catholic is in a public position and defiant about what he is doing as a Catholic, for example supporting abortion or approving of it, then that Catholic should be denied Eucharist by the person giving the sacrament during Mass.

Pope John Paul II explained this and Pope Benedict XVI did so as well when he was known as Cardinal Josef Ratzinger, president of the Congregation for the Doctrine of the Faith.[37] He was very clear in the 2004 memo he sent to the American bishops.[38] He sent the bishops that memo because the Church was and is painfully aware that, in the United States, there are many public figures who act in ways contrary to Catholic teaching and yet claim they are still Catholics in good standing. They arrogantly receive the Eucharist as though their involvement with sins like abortion doesn't really matter!

This is truly sad because, not only does it cause confusion among lay Catholics and the general public, but it jeopardizes the souls of these individuals as well. These are the types of public figures Pope Francis was referring to when he wrote that such "people cannot receive Holy Communion and at the same time act or speak against the commandments, in particular when abortions, euthanasia, and other serious crimes against life and family are facilitated."

It is this consistent respect for the Eucharist and the commitment to protect Christ from sacrilege that inspires us to thank God for Pope Francis. At the same time, we must pray for our American bishops and ask God to help them see the wisdom in making sure that the body of Christ is denied to any Catholic who uses his public position to advocate for or otherwise support abortion, euthanasia, homosexual marriage, or any of those things that are offensive to God and against the teachings of the Church.

The denial of the sacrament to those who are involved in promoting or committing such grave sins in public is a step toward healing—the healing of a soul sidetracked by sin. Denying the Eucharist to such people is not punishment; it is rather an act that protects the body of Christ and at the same time teaches the person in question that he needs to repent of his public advocacy of crimes against God's commandments.

Pope Francis' words spoken in his first homily really tell us why it is so important to walk with Christ, even though we might stumble on the way:[39]

> When one does not walk, one halts. When one does not build on stone what happens? That happens which happens to children on the beach when they make sand castles, it all comes down, it is without substance. When one does not confess Jesus Christ, I am reminded of the expression of Léon Bloy: *"He who does not pray to the Lord prays to the devil."* When one does not confess Jesus Christ, one confesses the worldliness of the devil, the worldliness of the demon.
>
> To walk, to build/construct, to confess. But the matter is not so easy, because in walking, in building, in confessing, at times there are shocks, there are movements that are not properly movements of the journey: They are movements that set us back.
>
> . . .
>
> When we walk without the cross, when we build without the cross, and when we confess Christ without the cross, we are not disciples of the Lord: We are worldly, we are bishops, priests, cardinals, popes, but not disciples of the Lord.
>
> I would like that everyone, after these days of grace, should have the courage, truly the courage, to walk in the presence of the Lord, with the cross

of the Lord; to build up the Church upon the blood of the Lord that was shed upon the cross; and to confess the only glory: Christ crucified. And in this way the Church will move forward.

Pope Francis: Apostle of hope

Hope is defined in the *Catechism of the Catholic Church* as one of the theological virtues. It is hope "by which we desire the kingdom of heaven and eternal life as our happiness, placing our trust in Christ's promises and relying not on our own strength, but on the help of the grace of the Holy Spirit."[40]

Pope Francis is, by his very life, a sign of hope and a teacher of what it means to hope in Christ. He wrote about this virtue,[41]

> You cannot acquire the virtue of hope by yourself; the Lord must give it to you. But another thing is how we use it, administer it, accept it.... The way we look at it, hope is one of the three theological virtues, along with faith and charity. We normally give more importance to faith and charity. However, hope is what structures our path in life. One danger is that we fall in love with the path and lose sight of the goal; another danger is quietism: To be looking at the goal and doing nothing on the path. Christianity has experienced times when there were powerful quietist movements. These go against the commandment of God which says that we have to transform the world, to work.

Pope Francis has already electrified many in the Church who have described his willingness to be with the people and for the people. He has spoken repeatedly with love and encouragement, no matter where he is preaching or talking with people.

During his inauguration Mass homily, he spoke of hope, saying,[42]

> In the second reading, Saint Paul speaks of Abraham, who, "hoping against hope, believed" (Rom 4:18). Hoping against hope! Today too, amid so much darkness, we need to see the light of hope and to be men and women who bring hope to others. To protect creation, to protect every man and every woman, to look upon them with tenderness and love, is to open up a horizon of hope; it is to let a shaft of light break through the heavy clouds; it is to bring the warmth of hope! For believers, for us Christians, like Abraham, like Saint Joseph, the hope that we bring is set against the horizon of God, which has opened up before us in Christ. It is a hope built on the rock which is God.

All of his sermons during the 2013 Easter celebration provided added examples of the kindness and love of mankind that he shares because hope is the essence of all that he says and does.

During the March 30, 2013, Easter Vigil homily, Pope Francis said:[43]

> Brothers and sisters, let's not close ourselves to the newness that God wants to bring to our lives! Often we are tired, disheartened, sad; we feel the weight of our sins and think we're not going to make it. Let's not get locked up in ourselves. Let's not lose our confidence. Let us never give up. There are no situations that God cannot change;

there is no sin that He won't forgive if we open ourselves to him.

And during his 2013 Easter homily he said:[44]

This same love out of which the Son of God became man and followed the way of humility and self-giving to the very end, down to hell—to the abyss of separation from God—this same merciful love has flooded Jesus' dead body with light and transfigured it; has made it pass into eternal life. Jesus did not return to his former life, to an earthly life, but entered into the glorious life of God and He entered there with our humanity, opening us to a future of hope.

This is what Easter is: It is the exodus, the passage of human beings from the slavery to sin and evil to the freedom of love and goodness. Because God is life, life alone, and we are His glory, the living person.

Dear brothers and sisters, Christ died and rose once for all time and for everyone, but the power of the Resurrection, this passing from the slavery to evil to the freedom of goodness, must be accomplished in every age, in our concrete existence, in our everyday lives. How many deserts, even today, do human beings need to cross! Above all, the desert within, when we are lacking love for God and neighbor, when we fail to realize that we are guardians of all that the Creator has given us and continues to give us. God's mercy can make even the driest land become a garden, can restore life to dry bones (cf. Ez. 37:1-14).

You might think that the vision of a dry, sandy desert does not apply to us, but I think it really does encapsulate how we feel when we think God has abandoned us or when we, sadly, have ignored Him. That desert of the soul can only be renewed through the virtue of hope. It is the spiritual horizon that Pope John Paul II described: "Man always has before him the spiritual horizon of hope, thanks to the *help of divine grace* and with *the cooperation of human freedom.*"[45]

The virtue of hope is a remarkable healer, restoring us to love of God and all His goodness.

The young people who heard the Holy Father talk about hope during his Wednesday, April 3, 2013, general audience were surely lifted up to renew their relationship with the Lord as well. On that day the pope said these words to the youth present in that hall:[46]

> Take this certainty to all, the Lord is alive and walks beside us in our lives. This is your mission. Take this hope forward with you. Be anchored to this hope, this anchor that is heaven. Hold tight to the lifeline. Be anchored and carry this hope forward. You, witnesses of Jesus, carry forward the testimony that Jesus is alive and that this will give us hope; it will bring hope to this world that has grown a bit old because of wars, evil, and sin. Young people, go forward!

Young people have been inspired by recent popes on many occasions including these words of love from Pope John Paul II:[47]

> Dear young people, the Church needs genuine witnesses for the new evangelization: Men and women whose lives have been transformed by meeting with Jesus, men and women who are

capable of communicating this experience to others. The Church needs saints. All are called to holiness, and holy people alone can renew humanity. Many have gone before us along this path of gospel heroism, and I urge you to turn often to them to pray for their intercession.

Pope Benedict XVI, whose love for the young was so apparent, told a group of them in 2011, "Dear young people, the Church depends on you! She needs your lively faith, your creative charity and the energy of your hope. Your presence renews, rejuvenates, and gives new energy to the Church."[48]

These examples of the inspiration hope can bring and the manner in which hope can brighten our lives lead us to believe that with spiritual leaders like Pope Francis, we can find our way to a closer and more personal friendship with God our Father.

Pope Francis, hope, and the homosexual person

The Holy Father has always been a servant to the poor and downtrodden; it is his way of teaching others by his example. There are many examples of this compassionate side of the Holy Father, but John-Henry Westen has written about one that may seem more than strange to some, though it is the epitome of Catholic faith in action. Westen writes:[49]

It may seem totally schizophrenic to some, but Pope Francis has indeed kissed[50] the feet of AIDS patients in an act of love and caring for those afflicted with the dreaded disease and he is also the same man who in no uncertain terms spoke of gay "marriage" as a machination of the devil.

But these stances are totally consistent with the Catholic view of "love the sinner but hate the sin." In fact, it is only love which in today's world can cause people to point with love to the harm which homosexual sex causes so that our brothers and sisters in that lifestyle can come to healing and life. It surely doesn't make you popular, it may very well get you in trouble with friends, family, work, and perhaps even the law, but out of love we speak the truth.

Some people do not understand Catholic teaching on homosexuality. The confusion arises because the media does not want the average person to see that it is quite possible, in fact required of us as Christians, to love the sinner always but never the sin. The pope is trying hard to teach that lesson as he did in the years prior to his election.

Homosexual marriage, also known as "same-sex marriage," "gay marriage," or "homosexual civil unions" was declared by then-Cardinal Bergoglio in July 2009 to be a "machination of the father of lies." He used this definition when he presented a declaration to his priests with a request that it be read at all Masses.[51]

Prior to the vote on same-sex marriage in Argentina in June of 2010, then-Cardinal Bergoglio wrote a particularly moving appeal to the Carmelite nuns asking for their prayers. His letter is so beautiful that we reprint it in full because it is a message that makes Catholic teaching so clear. The love, the hope, and the truth come alive in these words:[52]

Dear Sisters,

I write this letter to each one of you in the four monasteries of Buenos Aires. The Argentine people must face, in the next few weeks, a situation whose result may gravely harm the family. It is the bill on matrimony of persons of the same gender.

The identity of the family, and its survival, are in jeopardy here—father, mother, and children. The life of so many children who will be discriminated beforehand due to the lack of human maturity that God willed them to have with a father and a mother is in jeopardy. A clear rejection of the law of God, engraved in our hearts, is in jeopardy.

I recall words of Saint Thérèse when she speaks of the infirmity of her childhood. She says that the envy of the Devil tried to extort her family after her older sister joined the Carmel. Here, the envy of the Devil, through which sin entered the world, is also present, and deceitfully intends to destroy the image of God: Man and woman, who receive the mandate to grow, multiply, and conquer the earth. Let us not be naive: It is not a simple political struggle; it is an intention [which is] destructive of the plan of God. It is not a mere legislative project (this is a mere instrument), but rather a "move" of the father of lies who wishes to confuse and deceive the children of God.

Jesus tells us that, in order to defend us from this lying accuser, He will send us the Spirit of Truth. Today, the nation [patria], before this situation, needs the special assistance of the Holy Ghost that may place the light of truth amid the shadows of error; it needs this advocate who may defend us from the enchantment of so many sophisms with which this bill is being justified, and which confuse and deceive even people of good will.

That is why I turn to you and ask from you prayer and sacrifice, the two invincible weapons which Saint Thérèse confessed to have. Cry out to the Lord that He may send His Spirit to the senators who are to place their votes. That they may not do it moved by error or by circumstantial matters, but rather according to what the natural law and the law of God tell them. Pray for them, for their families; that the Lord may visit, strengthen, and console them. Pray that they may do great good for the nation.

This bill will be discussed in the senate after July 13. Let us look towards Saint Joseph, to Mary, the Child, and let us ask with fervor that they will defend the Argentine family in this moment. Let us recall what God himself told his people in a time of great anguish: "This war is not yours, but God's." That they may succor, defend, and accompany us in this war of God.

Thank you for what you will do in this struggle for the nation. And, please, I beg you, pray for me also. May Jesus bless you, and may the Blessed Virgin protect you.

Shortly after this letter was sent, homosexual marriage was legalized in Argentina. *Time* magazine reported, "Argentina's synod of bishops thundered similarly: 'This is not a private matter or a matter of religious choice, this is a reality rooted in the very nature of humanity, which is male and female.' And Cardinal Bergoglio, in a fresh declaration, prophesied that 'if approved, this law would be a real and dire anthropological throwback.'"[53]

Or, to put it another way, God's design for man and for woman and for the sanctity of marriage would be violated in a most dire way.

The following year, in his 2011 book *Sobre el cielo y la tierra* (*On heaven and earth*), Bergoglio wrote:[54]

> There have always been homosexuals. The island of Lesbos is known as a place where homosexual women lived. But never in history has anyone sought to give it the same status as marriage. Whether it was tolerated or not, whether it was admired or not, no one regarded it as equivalent. We know that in moments of great change, the phenomenon of homosexuality increased. But this is the first time that anyone posed the legal possibility of equating it with marriage. I regard it as a retrograde step, anthropologically speaking. I am saying this because it transcends the religious question; it is an anthropological one. If a union is private, no third parties or society are affected. But now that it has been given the status of marriage and given facilities for adoption, children will be affected. Everyone needs a masculine father and a feminine mother to help them shape their identity.

Even with all of this written down, some reporters arrogantly reported that Pope Francis endorsed same-sex civil unions, but one need only look at his history[55] as a dedicated teacher of Catholic doctrine and as a lover of poverty and simplicity to realize that his consistency in defending[56] Catholic teaching on homosexuality does not allow for exceptions on any aspect of legitimizing homosexual unions, no matter what you call them.

Whether it is homosexual marriage or the question of homosexuals in the priesthood, the teaching of the Church has never wavered.

Pope Francis is a man who has spent his entire priesthood delivering a consistent message that reflects Church teaching, and that includes the Catholic doctrine on homosexuality.

In conclusion

If there has ever been a doubt in your mind that we are living in the age of saintly men following in the steps of our first pope, St. Peter, it is my hope that this little book helps you see that what we have before us is a beautiful image of faith, hope, and charity.

It is heartening to know that because of our new pope's love for the poor, the marginalized, and so much more, many lapsed Catholics are experiencing a reversion to their Catholic faith. One woman said that the election of Pope Francis "was a sign. . . . It was like a miracle!"[57]

He is inspiring so many through his witness to the goodness of Christ and His love for all human beings without exclusion. Pope Francis is a living example of his namesake, St. Francis of Assisi. This is true particularly of Catholics who had lost trust in the Church because of the sex-abuse scandals and a sense that justice was lacking, even at times among members of the hierarchy. Now it is as though we have as a Church this amazing opportunity to begin again, refreshed and inspired.

There is so much that could be said about Pope Francis and his magnetism. His own words draw us to reflection, to a renewal of faith, and to a deeper love of our fellow human beings:[58]

> It is the Holy Spirit that we received in baptism that teaches us, leads us to say to God, "Father." Or rather, Abba Father. This is our God. He is a father to us. The Holy Spirit produces in us this new status as children of God, and this is the greatest gift we receive from the Paschal mystery of Jesus. And God treats us as His children, He understands us, forgives us, embraces us, loves us even when we make mistakes. In the Old Testament, the prophet Isaiah said that even though a mother may forget her child, God never, ever forgets us (cf. 49:15). And this is a beautiful thing, beautiful!

Pope Francis is the living portrait of holiness. His words and his actions coincide so beautifully, and for that we thank God.

Afterword
Part A

Below is a translation of then-Cardinal Bergoglio's Lenten message for Buenos Aires given on Ash Wednesday—exactly one month before his election to the papacy.[59]

To the priests, the consecrated, and the laity of the archdiocese,

Rend your hearts, not your garments;

Return now to the Lord your God,

Because He is compassionate and merciful,

Slow to anger and rich in mercy . . .

Little by little we get used to hearing and seeing, through the media, the black chronicle of contemporary society, presented almost with perverse enjoyment and we also get used to touching it and hearing it around us and in our own flesh. The drama is in the street, in the neighborhood, in our home, and, why not, in our heart. The suffering of the innocent and peaceful never ceases to hit us; contempt for the rights of the most fragile persons and peoples are not that foreign to us; the dominance of money with its demonic effects such as drugs, corruption, the trafficking of persons, including children, together with material and moral misery are the common currency. The destruction of fitting work, the painful emigrations and the lack of a future are also added to this symphony. Our errors and sins as Church are also not absent from this great panorama. The most personal egoisms are justified, and not because of this are they lesser, the lack of ethical values in a society that metastasizes in families, in the coexistence of neighborhoods, villages, and cities, speak to us of our limitation, of our weakness, and of our inability to transform this innumerable list of destructive realities.

The trap of impotence makes us think: Does it make sense to try to change this? Can we do anything in face of this situation? Is it worthwhile to try if the world continues its carnival dance disguising everything for a while? However, when the mask falls, the truth appears and, although for many it is anachronistic to say it, sin reappears, which wounds our flesh with all its destructive force, twisting the destinies of the world and of history.

Lent comes to us as a cry of truth and sure hope, which answers yes, that it is possible not to put on makeup and draw plastic smiles as if nothing is happening. Yes, it is possible that everything be made new and different because God continues to be "rich in kindness and mercy, always willing to forgive," and He encourages us to begin again and again. Today we are again invited to undertake a Paschal journey to truth, a journey that includes the cross and renunciation, which will be uncomfortable but not sterile. We are invited to admit that something is not right in ourselves, in society, and in the Church, to change, to turn around, to be converted.

Strong and challenging on this day are the words of the prophet Joel: Rend your hearts, not your garments: Be converted to the Lord your God. It is an invitation to all peoples; no one is excluded.

Rend your hearts, not your garments, artificial penance without guarantees for the future.

Rend your hearts, not your garments, formal and fulfilled fast which continues to keep us satisfied.

Rend your hearts, not your garments, superficial and egoistic prayer which does not reach the depth of our life to allow it to be touched by God.

Rend your hearts to say with the psalmist: "We have sinned." "Sin is the wound of the soul: Oh poor wounded one, recognize your Physician! Show him the wounds of your guilt. And given that our secret thoughts are not hidden from Him, make Him hear the groan of your heart. Move Him to compassion with your tears, with your insistence. Importune Him! May He hear your sighs, make your pain reach Him so that, in the end, He can say to you: The Lord has forgiven your sin" (Saint Gregory the Great). This is the reality of our human condition. This is the truth that can bring us closer to genuine reconciliation with God and with men. It is not about discrediting self-esteem but about penetrating the depth of our hearts and of assuming the mystery of suffering and pain which has bound us for centuries, thousands of years, always.

Rend your hearts, so that through that crack we can really look at ourselves.

Rend your hearts, open your hearts, because only in a broken and open heart can the merciful love of God enter, who loves and heals us.

Rend your hearts says the prophet, and Paul asks us almost on his knees, "Be reconciled with God." To change one's way of living is the sign and fruit of this broken and reconciled heart by a love that surpasses us.

This is the invitation, given the many wounds that harm us and that can lead us to the temptation of hardening us: Rend your hearts to experience in silent and serene prayer the gentleness of God's tenderness.

Rend your hearts to be able to love with the love with which we are loved, to console with the consolation that consoles us and to share what we have received.

The liturgical time that the Church begins today is not only for us, but also for the transformation of our families, our communities, our Church, our homeland, of the whole world. They are 40 days to be converted to the very holiness of God; to become collaborators who receive grace and the possibility to reconstruct human life so that every man will experience the salvation that Christ won for us with his death and resurrection.

Together with prayer and penance, as a sign of our faith in the strength of Easter which transforms everything, we also prepare to begin as in other years our "solidaristic Lenten gesture." As [a] Church in Buenos Aires that marches towards Easter and that believes that the

Kingdom of God is possible, we need to have spring from our hearts, broken by the desire of conversion and love, the grace and effective gesture that will alleviate the sorrow of so many brothers who walk with us. "No act of virtue can be great if it is not followed by advantage for others. So, no matter how much time you spend fasting, no matter how much you sleep on a hard floor and eat ashes and sigh continually, if you do no good to others, you do nothing great" (Saint John Chrysostom).

This Year of Faith we are living is also an opportunity that God gives us to grow and mature in our encounter with the Lord who makes Himself visible in the suffering face of so many youth without a future, in the trembling hands of the forgotten elderly and in the vacillating knees of so many families that continue to face life without finding anyone to support them.

I wish you a holy Lent, a penitential and fruitful Lent and, please, I ask you to pray for me. May Jesus bless you and the Holy Virgin look after you.

Paternally,
Cardinal Jorge Mario Bergoglio, S.J.
Buenos Aires, February 13, 2013,
Ash Wednesday

Part B

Below are insights on the views and actions of Pope Francis from fellow Americans:

Father John O'Brien, S.J., on his fellow Jesuit, Pope Francis:[60]

> The pope must be a martyr because the whole Church is called to be *martyrological*—that is, a living witness to Christ, and Christ crucified. Since Peter's foundational declaration, "You are Christ, the Son of the Living God," the Petrine office has primarily been about professing this living reality. Jesus responded to this first ecclesial "faith statement" by declaring that flesh and blood had not revealed this to Peter but the heavenly Father, and that Peter would be the rock on which He would build His Church. The Church, then, is built upon a public profession of faith. Peter becomes the first credo-bearer—or witness. But there is more.
>
> A witnessing pope will be a prophetic pope, one who speaks truth to power. The Church is always going to call humanity to the hidden truth of the cross: That in humility and self-gift reside life. The Church thus defies all attempts to place her in an ideological box. She will admonish and speak truth to tyranny and power whether on the right or the left. But she must be willing to do this to the end.

Jeffrey Mirus, commenting on then-Cardinal Bergoglio's message to his fellow cardinals just prior to the conclave, on the subject of problems in the Church, gave us these examples of "spiritual narcissism" among others:[61]

1. When theologians and academicians redefine faith and morals according to their own desires.

2. When laymen use the Church for their spiritual comfort while rejecting whatever Catholic teachings they do not like.

3. When people at any level in the Church decide they are not called to express the way, the truth, and the life of Christ to others because it is outside their personal comfort zone.

4. When cardinals and bishops refuse to speak truth to power, preferring to enjoy life with "people who matter," they are being narcissistic and self-referential, and they are making the Church sick.

5. Whenever anyone defines right and wrong in terms of chronology ("Come on, it's 2013! Don't be so medieval!").

6. When priests alter the liturgy to suit their tastes or fail to teach the fullness of Catholic doctrine.

Washington Post columnist Marc Thiessen gives advice to the Republican Party: Emulate Pope Francis![62]

> If Republicans want to convince Americans that they care, they need to emulate Francis and start showing up in the barrios and the inner cities. It's not enough for Republicans to simply vote for school choice; they need to spend time with students struggling in failing schools. It's not enough to rail against dependency; they need to spend time helping those trapped in dependency to get the skills they need to get off public

assistance. It's not enough to complain about Obama's class-warfare rhetoric; they need to spend time fighting for the vulnerable.

They don't have to abandon their principles to do it. As a cardinal, Bergoglio urged the faithful to "defend the unborn against abortion even if they persecute you, calumniate you, set traps for you, take you to court or kill you." But also he insisted that "no child should be deprived of the right to be born, the right to be fed, the right to go to school." Notice that he did not stop at the right to be born. Neither should Republicans. The GOP needs to put as much emphasis on ensuring that children are fed and educated as it does on their fundamental right to life.

Kristen Hatten, president of New Wave Feminists,[63] recently wrote,[64]

I know that as a Catholic, I look to the Holy Father as an example. Pope Francis gave up his limousine to ride the bus. He chose to live in a small apartment instead of the luxurious accommodations to which he was entitled. From the balcony at the Sistine Chapel, having just been announced the new pope; *he* bowed his head for *our* prayers. He knelt to wash the feet of the dying and outcast. "Go out," he told Argentine priests last year. "Go out and share your testimony, go out and interact with your brothers, go out and share, go out and ask. Become the Word in body as well as spirit."

I don't know a whole lot yet about Pope Francis. Like the rest of the world, I'll have to learn, and wait, and watch as he embarks on his pontificate.

But meanwhile, I know that his message of humility, love, and the dignity of the human person strengthens my resolve to be a pro-life Catholic committed to help, to understand, and not to condemn.

Pro-life congressman Chris Smith reflects[65] on Pope Francis' words:

> The pope's homily and his call to protect, invoking Our Lord's words in Matthew 25 about protecting the least of our brethren, was just an extraordinary rallying call to every one of us to reach out to the disenfranchised and the weakest and most vulnerable—whether it be the unborn child or women who are at risk . . . in all of our countries.
>
> Whatever the situation may be, we have to become protectors. That's what we're admonished to do by Our Lord and certainly we heard that today from Pope Francis.

A special hug for a special child

On Easter Sunday, as Pope Francis was being driven through the crowds, he noticed a little boy with special needs. The Holy Father stopped to embrace this child, a little boy named Dominic, who has cerebral palsy. Afterward, his father, Paul Gondreau, wrote about the experience:[66]

> This tender moment, an encounter of a modern Francis with a modern Dominic (as most know, tradition holds that St. Francis and St. Dominic enjoyed an historic encounter), moved not only my family (we were all moved to tears), not only

those in the immediate vicinity (many of whom were also brought to tears by it), not only by thousands who were watching on the big screens in the square, but by the entire world. Images of this embrace quickly went viral, and by Easter Sunday afternoon it was the lead picture on the Drudge Report, with the caption, "Change Hatred into Love" (a paraphrase of Pope Francis' *Urbi et Orbi* message that followed shortly thereafter), where it remains even as I write this.

And then Gondreau made a wise observation that encapsulates so much about a holy man few really understand. He wrote:

> One more thing. Pope Francis' embrace of my son, Dominic, indicates that we should not interpret the new pontiff's expressed devotion to the poor, already a cornerstone of his pontificate, in facile, purely material (let alone political) categories. His Easter embrace of my son stands out as a compelling witness to the kind of "poverty" that he urges us to adopt, the poverty that he pointed to in the opening line of his *Urbi et Orbi* message yesterday: "I would like [the message of Christ's resurrection] to go out to every house and every family, especially where the suffering is greatest." Parents of disabled children, stand up and find solace and encouragement in these simple yet profound words.

Holy Thursday 2013 controversy:
Washing the feet of ten men and two women

It is concerning to some who understand the traditional practice of the priest washing the feet of 12 men as part of the Holy Thursday ritual that Pope Francis included two women in the 12 whose feet he washed at the Casal del Marmo detention center.[67]

Associated Press reported, "Francis' decision to disregard Church law and wash the feet of two women—a Serbian Muslim and an Italian Catholic—during a Holy Thursday ritual has become something of the final straw, evidence that Francis has little or no interest in one of the key priorities of Benedict's papacy—reviving the pre-Vatican II traditions of the Catholic Church."[68]

This sounds a bit harsh, but it must be noted that canon lawyer Ed Peters took exception to it as well, pointing out that, although the ceremony involving the women might bear some good effects in the long run, it also sows even more confusion among the faithful. It leaves people wondering what might happen next in this papacy.[69]

Personally, the first thing I thought of was the pope's commitment to love, charity, and providing succor to the poor and disenfranchised. It is clear that, in his world experience, he has worked tirelessly to include all people in the compassion he exudes in sermons and daily actions. Recall chapter seven of St. Luke's gospel in which a woman came to Jesus as He was eating in the house of a Pharisee. She is noted in the gospel as a "sinner." This woman bent down and washed Christ's feet with her tears, dried them with her hair, kissed His feet, and rubbed them with fine oil.

When challenged about letting her do this, Christ said, "Many sins are forgiven her because she loved much." And to the woman He said, "Thy faith has saved you, go in peace."

One can see this same expression of mercy in the loving actions of Pope Francis.

Papal encyclicals and Church documents:

Pope John Paul II, *Familiaris Consortio* (*The role of the Christian family in the modern world*), 1981, http://www.vatican.va/holy_father/john_paul_ii/apost_exhortations/documents/hf_jpii_exh_19811122_familiaris-consortio_en.html.

Cardinal Joseph Ratzinger, *Conscience and Truth*, 1991, http://www.ewtn.com/library/CURIA/RATZCONS.HTM.

Pope John Paul II, *Veritatis Splendor* (*The Splendor of Truth*), 1993, http://www.vatican.va/holy_father/john_paul_ii/encyclicals/documents/hf_jp-ii_enc_06081993_veritatis-splendor_en.html.

Pope John Paul II, *Evangelium Vitae* (*The Gospel of Life*), 1995, http://www.vatican.va/holy_father/john_paul_ii/encyclicals/documents/hf_jp-ii_enc_25031995_evangelium-vitae_en.html.

Pope John Paul II, *Ecclesia de Eucharistia* (*The bond between the Church and the Eucharist*), 2003, http://www.vatican.va/holy_father/special_features/encyclicals/documents/hf_jp-ii_enc_20030417_ecclesia_eucharistia_en.html.

Cardinal Joseph Ratzinger, *Worthiness to Receive Holy Communion* (a memo to the members of the United States Conference of Catholic Bishops), 2004, http://www.ewtn.com/library/CURIA/cdfworthycom.HTM.

Congregation for the Doctrine of the Faith, *Dignitas Personae (The dignity of the person)*, 2008, http://www.vatican.va/roman_curia/congregations/cfaith/documents/rc_con_cfaith_doc_20081208_dignitas-personae_en.html.

Pope Benedict XVI, *Caritas in Veritate (Truth in love)*, 2009, http://www.vatican.va/holy_father/benedict_xvi/encyclicals/documents/hf_ben-xvi_enc_20090629_caritas-in-veritate_en.html.

Notes

1. "We are blessed to have so many documents written by Pope Benedict XVI; a complete list of documents can be found at the end of the book"

2. *Catechism of the Catholic Church Online*, s.v. "charity," accessed May 3, 2013, http://www.scborromeo.org/ccc/para/826.htm.

3. "Servants of the Lord and the Virgin of Matará," accessed May 3, 2013, http://ssvmusa.org/Events/CatholicCulture/Therese.Oct1.shtm.

4. Anugrah Kumar, "Pope Francis: Jesus, Not Pope at the Center of the Church," *The Christian Post*, March 17, 2013, http://www.christianpost.com/news/pope-francis-jesus-not-pope-at-the-center-of-the-church-92023/#wF5VLWR6UHTVG4p6.99.

5. Edward Pentin, "Pope: 'How I Wish for a Church that Is Poor and for the Poor!'" *National Catholic Register*, March 16, 2013, http://www.ncregister.com/blog/edward-pentin/pope-how-i-wish-for-a-church-that-is-poor-and-for-the-poor#ixzz2PY1qOIjh.

6. "Pope Francis' Sunday Homily at the Parish of St. Ann's in Vatican City," (a translation), *Zenit*, March 18, 2013, http://www.zenit.org/en/articles/pope-francis-sunday-homily-at-the-parish-of-st-ann-s-in-vatican-city.

7. Thomas G. Guarino, "Pope Francis and the Papacy," *First Things*, March 14, 2013, http://www.firstthings.com/onthesquare/2013/03/pope-francis-and-the-papacy.

8. *Wikipedia*, s.v. "Pope Francis," last modified May 4, 2013, http://en.wikipedia.org/wiki/Pope_Francis#Cardinal.

9. "Catholic Church in Argentine Republic (Argentina)," *GCatholic.org*, last modified May 4, 2013, http://www.gcatholic.org/dioceses/country/AR.htm.

10. David Uebbing, "Vatican TV Documentary Reveals Pope Francis' First Words," *EWTN News*, March 27, 2013, http://www.ewtnnews.com/catholic_news/Vatican.php?id=7330.

11. Cristian Martini Grimaldi, "Father for Everyone," *News.VA*, March 21, 2013, http://www.news.va/en/news/father-for-everyone.

12. Deacon Keith Fournier, "Pope Francis: Another Humble Man Named Francis Called to Rebuild the Church," *Catholic Online*, March 15, 2013, http://www.catholic.org/international/international story.php?id=50114.

13. Adelaide Darling, "Pope Francis Hailed by International Leaders," *EWTN News*, March 15, 2013, http://www.ewtnnews.com/catholic-news/World.php?id=7260#ixzz2PW9ZnFyS.

14. "Humility in the Church and the Fight against Corruption," *News.VA*, March 26, 2013, http://www.news.va/en/news/humility-in-the-church-and-the-fight-against-corru.

15. "Bergoglio's Intervention: A Diagnosis of the Problems in the Church," *Vatican Radio*, March 27, 2013, http://en.radiovaticana.va/news/2013/03/27/bergoglios_intervention:_a_diagnosis_of_the_problems_in_the_church/en1-677269speech.

16. Pope John Paul II, "Familiaris Consortio," *Vatican.VA*, November 22, 1981, http://www.vatican.va/holy_father/john_paul_ii/apost_exhortations/documents/hf_jp-ii_exh_19811122_familiaris-consortio_en.html.

17. "Letter of Pope Francis to Superior General of the Jesuits," *News.VA*, March 22, 2013, http://www.news.va/en/news/letter-of-pope-francis-to-superior-general-of-the.

18. *Deep Calls to Deep Blog*, "Can Pope Francis Renew Jesuit Education?" blog entry by Patrick Reilly, March 17, 2013, http://abyssum.wordpress.com/2013/03/17/is-it-too-much-to-ask-that-pope-francis-rescue-jesuit-educaton-from-the-scandal-that-it-has-become-after-the-vatican-council/.

19. Johann Christoph Arnold, "Finally a Francis," *Catholic Online*, March 16, 2013, http://www.catholic.org/national/national_story.php?id=50131.

20. "Pope Francis' Homily at Inauguration of Petrine Ministry Mass," *Zenit*, March 19, 2013, http://www.zenit.org/en/articles/pope-francis-homily-at-inauguration-of-petrine-ministry-mass.

21. Helen Hull Hitchcock, "Pope Francis: A Journey Begins," *National Review Online*, March 14, 2013, http://www.nationalreview.com/corner/342951/pope-francis-journey-begins-helen-hull-hitchcock.

22. "Pope Francis Has Lunch with Rome Priests," *News.VA*, March 30, 2013, http://www.news.va/en/news/pope-francis-has-lunch-with-rome-priests.

23. "Argentine Cardinal: Defend the Unborn unto Death," *Catholic News Agency*, September 5, 2005, http://www.catholicnewsagency.com/news/argentine_cardinal_defend_the_unborn_unto_death/.

24. Pope John Paul II, "Evangelium Vitae," *Vatican.VA*, March 25, 1995, http://www.vatican.va/holy_father/john_paul_ii/encyclicals/documents/hf_jp-ii_enc_25031995_evangelium-vitae_en.html.

25. Patrick B. Craine, "Pope Francis in 2005: Defend the Right to Life Even if They 'Have You Killed,'" *LifeSiteNews.com*, March 15, 2013, http://www.lifesitenews.com/news/pope-francis-back-in-2005-fight-abortion-even-if-they-take-you-to-court-or.

26. "St. Raymond Nonnatus," *Catholic Online*, accessed May 3, 2013, http://www.catholic.org/saints/saint.php?saint_id=314.

27. "10 Must-Read Quotations from Pope Francis: Portrait of a Forceful Thinker," *LifeSiteNews.com*, http://www.lifesitenews.com/news/10-must-read-quotations-from-pope-francis-portrait-of-a-forceful-thinker.

28. "I'm Seriously Loving this Guy," *Catholic News Live*, accessed May 3, 2013, http://catholicnewslive.com/story/70870.

29. John-Henry Westen, "As Cardinal, Pope Francis Strongly Condemned Abortion, Including in Rape Cases," *LifeSiteNews.com*, March 13, 2013, http://www.lifesitenews.com/news/as-cardinal-pope-francis-condemned-abortion-even-in-rape-cases.

30. Steven Ertelt, "Pope Francis Offers His Second Blessing to Pregnant Mom, Unborn Baby," *LifeNews.com*, March 14, 2013, http://www.lifenews.com/2013/03/14/pope-francis-offers-his-second-blessing-to-pregnant-mom-unborn-baby/.

31. Hugh Hewitt, "Pope Francis on 'God's Plan, Inscribed in Nature,'" *Hugh Hewitt*, March 19, 2013, http://www.hughhewitt.com/17802/.

32. Pope John Paul II, "Evangelium Vitae," *Vatican.VA*, March 25, 1995, http://www.vatican.va/holy_father/john_paul_ii/encyclicals/documents/hf_jp-ii_enc_25031995_evangelium-vitae_en.html.

33. Pope Benedict XVI, "Caritas in Veritate," *Vatican.VA*, June 29, 2009, http://www.vatican.va/holy_father/benedict_xvi/encyclicals/documents/hf_ben-xvi_enc_20090629_caritas-in-veritate_en.html.

34. Jerusalem Bible, Romans 13:10.

35. J.D.Long-Garcia, "Old Story about Then-Cardinal Bergoglio: 'Church Remains Sanctified through Eucharist,'" *The Catholic Sun*, March 13, 2013, http://www.catholicsun.org/2013/03/13/old-story-about-then-cardinal-bergoglio-church-remains-sanctified-through-eucharist/.

36. "New Pope: No Communion for Pro-Abortion Politicians," *Breitbart News*, March 13, 2013, http://www.breitbart.com/big-peace/2013/03/13/francis-no-communion-abortion.

37. Pope John Paul II, "Ecclesia de Eucharistia," *Vatican.VA*, April 17, 2003, http://www.vatican.va/holy_father/special_features/encyclicals/documents/hf_jp-ii_enc_20030417_ecclesia_eucharistia_en.html.

38. Pope Benedict XVI, "Worthiness to Receive Holy Communion: General Principles," *EWTN.com*, July 2004, http://www.ewtn.com/library/CURIA/cdfworthycom.HTM.

39. Robert Moynihan, "Letter 47: To Mary," *The Moynihan Letters*, March 14, 2013, http://themoynihanletters.com/from-the-desk-of/letter-47-to-mary.

40. *Catechism of the Catholic Church Online*, s.v. "hope," accessed May 3, 2013, http://www.scborromeo.org/ccc/para/1817.htm.

41. "Portrait of a Forceful Thinker," (excerpts from *Sobre el Cielo y la Tierra* by Pope Francis), *Mercator.net*, March 15, 2013, http://www.mercatornet.com/articles/view/portrait_of_a_forceful_thinker.

42. "Pope Francis' Homily at Inauguration of Petrine Ministry Mass," *Zenit*, March 19, 2013, http://www.zenit.org/en/articles/pope-francis-homily-at-inauguration-of-petrine-ministry-mass.

43. "Easter Vigil: Don't Be Afraid of God's Surprises. 'He Always Surprises Us!'" *Vatican Information Service*, March 31, 2013, http://visnews-en.blogspot.com/2013/03/easter-vigil-dont-be-afraid-of-gods.html.

44. "Pope Francis: God's Mercy Can Make Even the Driest Land Flower," *Vatican Information Service*, March 31, 2013, http://www.visnews-en.blogspot.com/2013/03/pope-francis-gods-mercy-can-make-even.html.

45. Pope John Paul II, "Veritatis Splendor," *Vatican.VA*, August 6, 1993, http://www.vatican.va/holy_father/john_paul_ii/encyclicals/documents/hf_jp-ii_enc_06081993_veritatis-splendor_en.html.

46. "Women Are the First Communicators of the Resurrection," *Vatican Information Service*, April 3, 2013, http://www.visnews-en.blogspot.com/2013/04/francis-women-are-first-communicators.html.

47. Pope John Paul II, "Message of the Holy Father John Paul II to the Youth of the World," *Vatican.VA*, August 2005, http://www.vatican.va/holy_father/john_paul_ii/messages/youth/documents/hf_jp-ii_mes_20040806_xx-world-youth-day_en.html.

48. Pope Benedict XVI, "Message of His Holiness Pope Benedict XVI for the 26th World Youth Day (2011)," *Vatican.VA*, http://www.vatican.va/holy_father/benedict_xvi/messages/youth/documents/hf_ben-xvi_mes_20100806_youth_en.html.

49. John-Henry Westen, "Pope Francis: Condemning Gay 'Marriage' While Kissing AIDS Patients' Feet," *LifeSiteNews.com*, March 18, 2013, http://www.lifesitenews.com/blog/pope-francis-condemning-gay-marriage-while-kissing-aids-patients-feet.

50. "Bringing Easter Hope to the Margins," *The Jesus Question Blog*, March 28, 2013, http://thejesusquestion.org/2013/03/28/bringing-easter-hope-to-the-margins/.

51. Matthew Cullinan Hoffman, "Homosexual 'Marriage' Is a Machination of the Devil, Argentinean Cardinal Warns," *LifeSiteNews.com*, July 9, 2010, http://www.lifesitenews.com/news/archive/ldn/2010/jul/10070902.

52. Robert Moynihan, "Letter 46: Pope Francis," *The Moynihan Letters*, March 13, 2013, http://themoynihanletters.com/from-the-desk-of/letter-46-pope-francis.

53. Uki Goñi, "Defying Church, Argentina Legalizes Gay Marriage," *Time*, July 15, 2010, http://www.time.com/time/world/article/0,8599,2004036,00.html#ixzz2OrAmRup2.

54. "Portrait of a Forceful Thinker," (excerpts from *Sobre el Cielo y la Tierra* by Pope Francis), *Conclaveblog*, March 15, 2013, http://conclaveblog.wordpress.com/2013/03/15/portrait-of-a-forceful-thinker/.

55. Elizabeth Lev, "So, What's in a Name?" *Zenit*, March 14, 2013, http://www.zenit.org/en/articles/so-what-s-in-a-name.

56. John-Henry Westen, "Pope Francis Will Never Approve Homosexual Civil Unions," *LifeSiteNews.com*, March 22, 2013, http://www.lifesitenews.com/news/pope-francis-will-never-approve-homosexual-civil-unions.

57. Tracy Connor, "'It Was a Sign': Lapsed Catholics Lured Back by Pope Francis," *NBCNews.com*, April 10, 2013, http://usnews.nbcnews.com/ news/2013/04/10/17671252-it-was-a-sign-lapsed-catholics-lured-back-by-pope-francis.

58. "Living Like God's Children," *News.VA*, April 10, 2013, http://www.news.va/en/news/audience-living-like-gods-children-full-text.

59. "Cardinal Bergoglio's Lenten Message for Buenos Aires," *Zenit*, March 14, 2013, http://www.zenit.org/en/articles/cardinal-bergoglio-s-lenten-message-for-buenos-aires.

60. John O'Brien, S.J., "From a Fellow Jesuit: Why the Pope Must Be a Martyr," *LifeSiteNews.com*, March 14, 2013, http://www.lifesitenews.com/news/from-a-fellow-jesuit-why-the-pope-must-be-a-martyr.

61. Jeff Mirus, "Spiritual Worldliness: Pope Francis' Critique of the Church," *CatholicCulture.org*, March 27, 2013, http://www.catholicculture.org/commentary/otc.cfm?id=1066.

62. Marc A. Thiessen, "What Republicans Can Learn from Pope Francis," *The Washington Post*, March 25, 2013, http://articles.washingtonpost.com/2013-03-25/opinions/37995838_1_pope-francis-cardinal-jorge-mario-bergoglio-republicans.

63. New Wave Feminists, http://www.newwavefeminists.com/.

64. Kristen Hatten, "What the Election of Pope Francis Means to Me as a Pro-Life Catholic," *Live Action News*, March 13, 2013, http://liveactionnews.org/what-the-election-of-pope-francis-means-to-me-as-a-pro-life-catholic/.

65. "U.S. Congressman: Pope Calls Us to Be Protectors," *News.VA*, March 19, 2013, http://www.news.va/en/news/us-congressman-pope-calls-us-to-be-protectors.

66. Paul Gondreau, "The Day Pope Francis Embraced My Disabled Son," *LifeSiteNews.com*, April 3, 2013, http://www.lifesitenews.com/news/the-day-pope-francis-embraced-my-disabled-son.

67. Laura Smith-Spark, "Pope Francis Washes Youths' Feet at Detention Center," *CNN*, March 28, 2013, http://www.cnn.com/2013/03/28/world/europe/vatican-pope.

68. "Pope's Foot-Wash a Final Straw for Traditionalists," *USA Today*, March 30, 2013, http://www.usatoday.com/story/news/world/2013/03/30/popes-upsets-traditionalists/2037463/.

69. "Some Thoughts on the VPO Statement Regarding the Mandatum Rite Controversy," *In the Light of the Law Blog*, April 1, 2013, http://canonlawblog.wordpress.com/2013/04/01/some-thoughts-on-the-vpo-statement-regarding-the-mandadtum-rite-controversy/.